WINTER

WINTER

Patricia Fargnoli

The Hobblebush Granite State Poetry Series, Volume VI

HOBBLEBUSH BOOKS

Brookline, New Hampshire

Composed in Adobe Arno Pro at Hobblebush Books

Printed in the United States of America

ISBN: 978-1-939449-01-6
Library of Congress Control Number: 2013948538

Cover photograph: *Cabin Door* by Edward Byrne of Oak Grove Photography
http://www.flickr.com/photos/94284791@N05/

Page 63, "Glosa": Lines from "In Memory of the Spanish Poet Federico Garcia Lorca," by Thomas Merton, from *The Collected Poems of Thomas Merton*, copyright ©1944 by Our Lady of Gethsemani Monastery. Reprinted by permission of New Directions Publishing Corp.

The Hobblebush Granite State Poetry Series, Volume VI
Editors: Sidney Hall Jr. and Rodger Martin

HOBBLEBUSH BOOKS
17-A Old Milford Road
Brookline, New Hampshire 03033
www.hobblebush.com

for Roger Dayton Jones
1934–2013

in memory and with love

CONTENTS

I

II

III

somehow, in some ways,
it has managed to survive—
pampas grass in the snow

—MATSUO BASHO

I

SHOULD THE FOX COME AGAIN TO MY CABIN IN THE SNOW

Then, the winter will have fallen all in white

and the hill will be rising to the north,

the night also rising and leaving,

dawn light just coming in, the fire out.

Down the hill running will come that flame

among the dancing skeletons of the ash trees.

I will leave the door open for him.

HUNGER

It is the gnawing within the silence
of the deep body which is like
the pool a waterfall replenishes
but can never fill.
The watery room of the body
and its voices who call and call
wanting something more, always more.

Once in a dream, the trees in a peach orchard
called out saying: Here, this bright fruit,
hold its roundness in your palm,
and I held one, wanting
the others I could not hold,
as the light fell through the trees,
one cascade after another.

Now, the wind from the hurricane
that veered out to sea,
and the hard rain blow through the space
where yesterday men felled the spruce,
its height and beauty, for no good reason.
Where it was, only emptiness remains,
and the stump level with the ground.

The wind finds its own place
and waits there holding its breath
for a moment, calling to no one,
surprising us by its stillness,
surprising even the rain which comes in
to my house through the untidy gardens
where it has been sending its life breath
over the dying mint and blood-red daylilies.

Summer is dying and I grow closer
to the shadow moving toward me
like the small spiders
that inhabit and hunt in the corners.
And the wind stirs, rattles the panels,
singing its own hunger, its own water song.

STILL, SILENCE MOVES ME TO SPEAK

of past, future, all those years
when life seemed ordinary
and was not. More wanderings

luminous memories
and the goat of chaos
always at cliff's edge
with his yellow burning eyes.

≈

The future burns on a short wire,
comes swiftly as lightning,
no dance can stop it.

≈

The dead visit my house
again and again.
They roam the old rooms.
What I am given in sleep—

scent of raspberries and lime,
a wooden chair rocking,
the blacksmith who thrusts
iron into the fire.

OLD MAN WEARING VEGETATION

after a photograph by Riitta Ikonen and Karoline Hjorth

He stands in a salt marsh up to his knees in the black water.
Around him sedges and rushes grow waist high.
Over his shoulders he wears a long shawl of cord grass
which with one arm he clasps to his chest like armor.
He might be pledging allegiance
to the natural world he stands on.
Thinning brown hair plastered on his forehead.
Gray beard. Squint-lines around his eyes.

≈

When I was a child I would go
into the fields behind our house and lie down
in tall timothy and sedges.
Hidden there, my body pressed a little circle
into the grass. All I could see
was the blue of sky above me
and those otherworldly beings the clouds
that were always trailing
across my vision to somewhere else
like a movie about almost nothing.

≈

The man of the marsh is not a god.
He has not stepped out of folklore,
is not part of a myth—
only an old man who has been talked into
standing there draped with what has been

pulled up from the marsh.
The photographer's vision. He
is transforming into landscape
the way at the end we all become
marsh grass, cumulus, sky.

February Pre-Dawn

inspired by "LaNoche," Anselm Hollo

Dark losing its grip   thin line of apricot sky in the west
beyond the crisscrossed   trunks of trees

in these apartments   there are not yet lights
a jumble of houses over there   in the village

old snow   that cold village like a white cat stalking the day
Soon   the sleeping will awake

and rise drowsily into the long lists
what's necessary   what's less necessary

Winter Grace

If you have seen the snow
under the lamppost
piled up like a white beaver hat on the picnic table
or somewhere slowly falling
into the brook
to be swallowed by water,
then you have seen beauty
and know it for its transience.
And if you have gone out in the snow
for only the pleasure
of walking barely protected
from the galaxies,
the flakes settling on your parka
like the dust from just-born stars,
the cold waking you
as if from long sleeping,
then you can understand
how, more often than not,
truth is found in silence,
how the natural world comes to you
if you go out to meet it,
its icy ditches filled with dead weeds,
its vacant birdhouses, and dens
full of the sleeping.
But this is the slowed-down season
held fast by darkness
and if no one comes to keep you company
then keep watch over your own solitude.
In that stillness, you will learn
with your whole body
the significance of cold
and the night,
which is otherwise always eluding you.

The Horse

I let the horse into my apartment,
pushed back chairs,
shoved the rattan chest
up against the tall bookcases,
moved photos of my grandchildren,
the clay bowl, Zuni fetishes.

I brushed his mane and his tail,
I curried him all over until he shone
like black rain on the edge of ice.
I fed him oats in a gold bucket.

He was a silent horse.
His old-soul eyes seemed to speak.
But if you came to visit
you wouldn't know he was there.
He was that quiet.

He smelled like sweat and leather,
and desire for the fields
which I knew I must return him to
though I wanted badly to keep him.

Horses Seen from a Distance

The quiet things that are

                in the silence of horses—
the six chestnut Morgans on the hill,

their necks in great bows to the earth,
their muzzles deep in the timothy grass.

I remember the curve of their withers
and how they grazed quietly in the distance

that day in the summer of my sadness
when I was driving

            to some forgotten destination.
One quick image my eyes took in—

                a snapshot only—
but through all time since, I still see them.

I don't know why

            they have stayed in my mind—
they were just part of the landscape—
and now

        I have gone so far beyond them.

WHEN WILL THE COWS COME HOME?

When the river freezes over and the pot boils
When the cat leaves the corner, when the tulips leave the bed

After absence has made your heart grow fonder
After apples have fallen far from the tree

Where the village is sleeping, the cows will come to the barn
Swishing their long tails, nodding their heads

If you have been waiting too long, the cows will come for you
If you believe in cows, they will come to your hand

If you hold out sweet grass in the late afternoon's last hour
From the greener pastures, they will surely come to you

After what has gone around, must come around,
They will come home

After the cat's nine lives are through and the dog's bone is buried
After the wishbone's been broken and the turkey's been eaten

Go with the flow of the river, the cows will come home
After your actions have spoken louder than words

Before all good things have come to an end
Before all the bridges have burned

The cows will come home

If the rolling stone has gathered its moss and is still
If the salt has been thrown over the barn's shoulder

All things come to those who wait

Cometh the hour, cometh the cows

Better late than never, everything in its own good time
The cows will come home

To your barn shaking their bells
They will come home to you

THE LETTER

In the bottom drawer of my desk I came across a letter that first arrived twenty-six years ago.
—TOMAS TRANSTRÖMER, "ANSWERS TO LETTERS"

I discover the envelope beneath the mattress.
Who knows how long it has been there?
As I unfold it and read it slowly, the rain-light

enters the window and my body,
light soft as gray linen, blurring the present.
Time is a thread wound around a spool

as if the past is in the room
only inches away from the present.
Would life have been different if I had answered?

It delivers its old love words to me again—
like waves sprawling over each other to reach the shore
or deer bounding across the road on a fall morning—

as though I have been waiting for them a long time,
though in truth I have gone on with my life,
other loves woven and torn, long swaths of solitude.

Did the night it was written hum
with the voices of cicadas, a marble moon?
Did the lover search the sky for an answer?

THE WEIGHT

Four times a day and twice during the night
through all of the relentless
ice-locked mid-winter days,

my widow-neighbor carries her dog,
a little honey-colored mutt,
down the stairs from her second floor apartment

into the sharp zero cold.
It's actually more like lugging an inert body,
Neddie his name is, old now and ill.

He whines and she knows
something is hurting badly.
Soon she will have to put him to sleep,

she can't do this much longer, old herself,
his weight unsteadying her on the steep stairs.
She cries while she tells me this,

as she lowers him down
to the ice-covered snow,
where he turns and turns, slipping a little

before he finally settles down,
the lemon juice stain spreading out
across the whiteness.

She says she's fighting off grief,
and not for the first time,
then stretches her back,

tired as it is, and bends to lift him again,
smoothing his long fur
with the practiced strokes of a lover.

PITY

In Blake's watercolor a woman lies at sea's edge,
arms across breasts, eyes and mouth open,
blonde curls rippling out beneath her body.

Two blind horses float mid-air their legs stretched
as if galloping, on their backs two angels.

The first one has leaned down and is lifting
a miniature body with its arms raised—
a soul? she has pulled from the dead woman.

I remember how when word came of the accident—
a close friend, mountain curve deadly with ice—
in my grief, what I wanted most to know

was where he went—the animating spirit—the one who sent
his poem about lake weeds tangled around his oar,
who, one hot August day by the ocean,

brought me his bandana dipped in cool water,
who found love after years of sadness, who had plans.
Where did he go with his many plans?

The painting's washed in quiet blues, the horses filmy white
like cirrus. The first angel's face glows with compassion.
The other stands with her back toward us,

arms stretched to the sides as far as possible
shielding the scene and this delicate operation
as though it needs her otherworldly protection.

Something enormous seems at stake.
Against all doubt, something is being born
from the dead woman's shrouded body.

GALWAY

after Tranströmer's "Track"

Thousands of crows flew through the Irish dusk
toward the copse of dark plane trees not far from here,
between the university and the famous river,

as when memories wing in from your past
with their loud continuous cawing
and then move beyond you, you don't know where.

Or as when someone dies and her spirit rises
to join the others who are leaving the world's sadness
to find a resting place in the quiet night branches beyond you.

The crows streamed past the high clerestory windows.
Dusk. The small wood they entered. The silver river.

WINTER

On the high hills, six white horses eat gray sky.
Snow has fallen, soft as flannel on the stoney road.
A wrong turn has taken me to this lost place.
In my jacket pocket, coins left through seasons
waiting for some felt future, some frivolous dream.
At what cost does one let coins fall, let losing come?

The road dead-ends in dense forest, deep as my life.
No one in the cabin there, no one in the woodshed, cold night fast.
Soup cans in the cupboard, a capable fire in the iron stove.
All alone here. I will be answering your letter for a long time.

II

THE PRECIOUS BOOK

Gwen John, circa 1920, oil on canvas

Who among us becomes what we set out to be?
The girl in the long blue dress cradles the open book
in a handkerchief in her hands. Next to her on the table,
an empty white plate and a closed black book
that partly extends over the edge of the table
as if she had just put it away and taken up this other.
The book she is reading is red and the girl's face is as devout
as a nun praying. The background, only a beige wall, nothing else.
Do the words of the valuable book enter her mind and change her?
Does she grow into the woman the artist later becomes?
A model for Rodin, his lover, that sad affair,
how she died overshadowed, unrecognized?
The red book is the only thing of bright color here, a light
in her hands. We give our hearts to her, don't we?
The long blue dress of her life, this moment of stasis
when the future can't touch her.

BIOGRAPHY FROM SEVENTY-FOUR

Once she knew a blind woman
who told her
the dreams of the blind
are full of voices and sound,
the touch of skin on skin—
velvet and satin,
footsteps coming and going,
a hundred bird calls
and the well of darkness.
Her bedroom is small and closed in.
One window, a bureau,
a nightstand piled with books
and a lamp with bad wiring
that flits on and off.
Years ago in a bedroom
with a green light bulb
she spent many afternoons with a man.
Love is a house afire,
a truck full of apples,
a stream with shining water.
Here is a secret:
most days she sleeps
most of the day.
She is not who she was.
Last week, she dreamt
she could still run.
She ran and ran a long way.
She sleeps uneasily now,
waking and turning,
waking and turning.

If she could be anywhere
she'd be on the windjammer
sailing to Martinique,
the one she remembers
that comes back in dreams,
the sea dark blue and rolling,
that paradise, green mountain
and white sand in the distance.
Don't go back to sleep now.
Love is the sun going down.
She regrets not having been
a better mother.
When she was a child, her mother
sang her to sleep.
The last song always
good night ladies
I have to leave you now.
Her fine hair, a flame
wrapped around her head.
Her green eyes.
Suddenly, unannounced,
death comes.
Love, a map with no roads,
no boundaries,
wild and full of grace.
Grace: what is given
without being asked,
what makes one able to rise.
The last time she felt joy

so long ago she can't remember.
She is afraid
of thunder that comes too close,
war and the threat of war.
She tries to protect herself
from the wind of no good.
Her name means *noble*.
She's done the best she could.

Notions

after Charles Wright

On my feet all day
in Sage-Allens notions department,
I spent college vacations selling bright
spools of thread, silvery needles, pins,
patterns, hoops for embroidery.
I learned how to ring the cash register,
its ching-chang whamming the drawer
into my middle, how to stamp charge cards,
how to send big bills flying in containers
up the pneumatic tubes to get change.
Downtown Hartford, a dollar an hour, 1957.
In our required navy skirts and white blouses,
my co-workers, old ladies,
reeked of Emeraude and Evening in Paris,
their powdery faces like wrinkled cotton.
We ignored each other,
                    from them I learned nothing.
Who knew where they went at night?
I was wrapped in my own after-work life,
third floor walk-up flat,
its railroad rooms: living room
sleeper couch that rolled out
without being asked,
kitchen I played hooky to paint egg-yolk yellow,
the bed with one end
that tipped up when you sat on it,
pale linoleum, its ground-in dirt,
no marriage,
three-month not-yet child
(about whom I had told no one)
gathering life in my belly.

FATHER POEM: A COLLAGE

in memory of Edouard Henri Boudreau, 1906–1947

My father is driving Old Betsy down to Doylestown
from Hartford. Rain pours so hard it leaks
in around the door and soaks my Girl Scout oxfords.
Nothing beyond the windshield but rain
and the car slides crazy around the highway.
Somewhere out there is New York City,

far beyond it, the woman I've not yet met
who will become my stepmother.
The car lurches. I am scared to death.

≈

Winter, near Christmas. A light comes on
in the cold bedroom where I have been sleeping.

Someone has woken me because he can't wait for morning.
My father who has just returned has entered
the room alone. He pulls the doll from her hiding place

beneath his coat which still smells of falling snow.
Her hair, dark braids, her dress shines in blue satin
as if she were made of stars.

≈

Why did you choose the Merchant's Hotel,
how long did you plan,
how did you get there?
What did the room look like,
did you call anyone,

had you asked for help,
was it day or night?
Where did you find the rope,
from what did you hang it,
did you stand on a chair?
What did you look like after?
Did you ever falter?
Wasn't I enough to keep you here?
Didn't you ever think of me?

≈

You were there and then missing.
The terror after which the body is torn
and the darkness enters it.

Dark night of your own dark soul father,
        don't you still ride my spirit?
            Black horse, black horse galloping.

≈

My father arrives cradling bread in his arms.
A round loaf, warm still,
and full of its own incense.

When he offers it, I take it from his hands and eat the mountain,
eat the garden of secrets. All the lamps of the village come on
as if they were voices out of time.

≈

On visitations, the way to somewhere else,
he'd stop off with me at the Hotel Bond,

mold smell of wallpaper, dust,
open whiskey bottle on the dresser.

Or at the PX, he'd sit at the bar
talking to the bartender
while I waited at a round table,
a glass of Coke—
                    a long wait.

Or the Rosewood Restaurant,
where all the waitresses flirted with him.
Everyone knew his name.

                    ≈

Emperor Penguin fathers sit on top of the nests.
Wolf fathers hold, feed, protect and play with their pups.
Dolphin fathers help in the care of the young.
The male bear sometimes kills and eats his young.

                    ≈

I answered the phone and the operator said
call from Pennsylvania.

I was ten and I knew only one person
who would call from Pennsylvania.

Daddy I said, and the man said who is this?
I said Daddy stop teasing, the man said
is there an adult there?

                    ≈

you won't undo what you did, you won't ever

be back

you knew this, you did it anyway.

≈

But once—

at Riverside Park I rode a white horse
with a dark-seed eye
and reins I held and the music played.
As you stood by,
the calliope played with a jangabell sound
"Till We Meet Again."

Father who will not be made small in me ever.

EIGHTH GRADE GRADUATION PARTY

It was the year the hay mower cut off the leg
of my orange cat, Cookie, the year we walked
over to the neighbors on Friday nights to watch
Arthur Godfrey in color on their new TV.

In Korea, our boys were fighting along the 38th parallel.
Truman fired MacArthur, *Kiss Me Kate* was on Broadway,
Count Turf won the Derby, and Johnny Ray
was making girls scream and cry across America.

Thirty of us out at night, most for the first time.
The Wilson firehouse, top floor strung with scraggly
blue streamers, suspended silver stars.
Record player at one end, punch bowl at the other.

It was the night I felt love for the first time.
Excitement at being out, a warm body glow
that seemed to emanate from me and permeate everything,
the boys clustered at one end horsing around, poking each other,

girls standing along the wall dying for an invitation that never came.
No boy in his right mind would ask a girl to dance
and risk ridicule. No boy did. The records played on: "Tennessee Waltz,"
"How High the Moon." Pair by pair, the girls ventured

out onto the floor to dance with each other.
Best friends, Pat Puccino and I both liked
Nicky Correnti, his friendly eyes,
the way he slicked back his brown hair with a comb.

Hadn't we jockeyed all spring to be on his team
in the after-school sandlot softball game?
Hadn't we got caught writing
our initials in chalk with his all over the cement

retaining wall in front of the school?
Now, Nicky ignored us, so we danced together
to the fast ones, the slow ones,
raced to get to the floor each time our song was played,

They tried to tell us we're too young,
too young to ever be in love,
singing along with King Cole's buttery voice,
all those words that got it exactly right.

RIDING THE COG RAILWAY UP MOUNT WASHINGTON

Mid-July, mid-way, fog closes in, the blue car rocks,
our bodies jostle back and forth.
You beside me, we are closed in
a world with strangers
riding at a thirty-seven degree angle, gravity pressing
our backs against the wooden slats.
The train, pushed by the engine, inches its way
upward toward the summit.
This is the only vacation we will ever take together,
the only time you have dared leave your doctors,
the cache of pills that keep
your mind on an even keel.
Beyond the windows, white and muted light
as we travel through clouds that are all we can see—
a wet gauze, ghostly wraps, the thin
blind milk covering a blind eye.
Around us the passengers stir, rustle,
a child cries.
You, who have always loved trains,
turn to me excited, whisper something,
but I can barely hear you over the racket
of wheels straining against the track
and the whoosh of the coal-fired engine.
The cold air gets colder. Rain
pounds against the car.
What is hidden out there: sheer drop-offs
to thousand-foot valleys?
Suddenly the engineer like some Norse god
in yellow oilcloth bursts through the door,

and the wind and the rain blast in with him.
The metal door, caught by the rush,
slam-clanks shut behind him.
Rain rolls off his slicker,
his wet face, his beard.
The air crackles: what message
of danger does he bring?
Wind yowls like a devil's child, the train clings
to tracks on a high trestle.
But he means only to tell us how far we've come,
how steep the incline, how far there is to go.
I lean into your shoulder.
Against the elements we hold on.
Rain on the edge of ice hurls bullets
against the windows.

NIGHT THOUGHTS

What pain did I see in your eyes
and still something beautiful inside?

My fear that you will go—
because no one stays forever.

This memory: at the outdoor café near the sea,
the waiter's black shirt

and some stranger waving to another stranger,
waving.

Lives move on like the shadows of windblown willows
to other lives.

Wounds heal but the scars remain vulnerable.
Sand sifts across the high dunes endlessly.

My body turns and turns again moving in and out of sleep,
dreams like sand dollars sinking.

SIXTY YEARS AFTER MY MOTHER'S DEATH

Her voice is nothing
but wind through a tunnel
beneath a snow-covered mountain
somewhere in the high country
a tunnel over tracks
where a train has just rattled through
a brief flash of lighted windows and passengers
on the way to the emptiness of the plains—
so that the tunnel is filled with absence
except for this wind that does not howl
but whispers as if she were bearing
her vestige back to me.

Depression

after Ruth Stone's "Euphoria"

This endless sadness,
this drizzle on the last day of September,
these words that pour as slowly as iced syrup.
Not even the small children of my children,
the pink and white balloons,
and the weekend party could lift it from me.
And where are those days
that return so often in dream?
The old houses with their light-held rooms,
the northern lake filled with perch and sunset,
summers in Smith's field, its tall grass oceans,
the lilac, purple clouds Pete and I climbed through,
the infant mice we couldn't save from the neighbor,
the night train whistling by like the boy
in the dark, calling the future
down by the long, long ago river.

Advice for the Sleeping Lady

Look at you. Again you have been sleeping
past night's end, shutting out the day
for which you have planned nothing.
Sleep, too much of it, your one great flaw.
Here's an idea: rise
from the three pillows and heated blanket,
and simply go
in your pink heart-printed pajamas
to the catacombs beneath Paris,
the *Empire of the Dead*.
So what if it's illegal.
A party waits there just for you.
Bring red wine and cheese for the cataphiles,
one chunk for the rat
that will certainly show, dragging its tail,
twitching its whiskers.
No one will know who you are
so be anybody, be Keats with his white hands,
Persephone hot for Hades, Eve
in a withering fig leaf that's about to fall.
Better yet go wearing a headlamp,
carrying a handwritten map,
and settle alone in a corner
in the narrow tunnel, near the moldy
stacks of bone. Settle into silence
deeper than any you've ever known.
A little scary isn't it, this death thing—a little morbid
but sleep is brother to death the ancients told us.
You'll feel right at home.

AT ALLEN BROTHERS GARDEN CENTER

for John Hodgen

Things happen to me, John said yesterday
about driving through Boston traffic,
the people in the next car
rolling down their window,
the woman with the bloody cheek
urgently asking where Charles Street, Mass General was,
and he, not from around there, not able to help.

      I think nothing happens to him
except the kinds of things that happen
to all of us, only he pays attention,
imbues everything with meaning.

      And because I am still thinking about that
today, the day after his reading, when I
am in Allen Brothers looking for flowers
and for basil to plant in a new clay pot,
I bend to study a monarch, its wings
faded, which has paused on a yellow flower
I forgot to notice the name of.
I am noticing how the proboscis
slips into the flower when an elderly woman
comes toward me, and because

                      I am also thinking
about my friend and connections between strangers,
I smile at her, say: *Look, a monarch, how beautiful.*
But she intones: *They are all dying—*
the butterflies, the bees, the birds. It's the poison they put
on the flowers—it kills everything. She's got this kind
of blank madness in her eyes, an emptiness,

so that I back away from her, wander over to
the geraniums. She follows me, stares, says
In the drama-heavy voice of an oracle:
Buy food, buy water.
I'm not crazy. Store food, store water. The Lord
is coming.
                    Around us, tables crowded with every kind
of annual and perennial. Above us, hang pots
of bleeding hearts, of petunias. There are
flats of purple and yellow pansies,
green hoses coiled on the dirt floor.
Moisture permeates the air—a kind of rough Eden.
Store food, store water, she urges again,
Even Glen Beck says so. You must listen.
The Lord is coming.
                         Which makes me think
of the Mayan calendar
that may or may not end this year.
I buy two geraniums and the basil
and escape from her, but I am wondering
whether in her cellar there are bottles
and bottles of water, shelves and shelves
of canned beans and tomatoes—
wondering whether she can sleep at night
knowing the end is coming, trying to save
the honey bees and monarchs and the poor birds
that are falling to their deaths every day from the poisons,
trying to save herself and the world from its own craziness.
        I think of my friend driving in heavy traffic
and the woman and her son in the next car hollering

Charles Street—Charles Street—as though Charles Street
were the one place that could save them,
how John believed that he had been singled out
to help and felt guilty because he could not,
the way I felt singled out to respond
to this old woman and failed,
the way we'd like to save the world.
But I fear that in the long run,
we cannot save each other even if we want to—
though I want to believe we can, at least sometimes,
so I drive home and carry in the geraniums.
And I fill a pot with the organic soil I've bought
and plant the basil and water it and trust it will grow.

Bellows Falls

The town's a ruin.
I think the landscape's made it so.
Hemmed in on the east:
the steep cliffside of Fall Mountain
glowers like a forehead casting its shadow.
And then the Connecticut River, and the broken
Vilas Bridge, barricaded for years.
Hemmed in on the west: that steep bank
and the hills that block the sunset.
Three times, they've tried to bring it back
entrepreneurs calling in architects, artists,
forming committees, renovating whole blocks,
then giving up; energy and money running out.

Go in morning's snow-encrusted light.
Cross Arch Bridge over the river
and watch the water boiling below the dam
yellow-white and dangerous.
When you get to Main,
(rattle of the freight train passing near)
let zero cold sharpen your cheeks and mind.

Not many books in Books on Village Square.
The clothing store's long gone
though at This and That
you might buy a mug with a kitten on it.
And the Good Buy's aisles explode with the used
plastic pocketbooks, dusty pants and blouses.
You could stop into Mountain View Tattoo,
but don't. Linger instead
before Coyote Moon, its windowful

of necklaces from Africa and China.
Too early for Smokin' Joe Chili
or a beer at the Hula Cat,

but go to Miss Bellows Falls Diner
for a second breakfast of bagel and bacon.
The smell of grease and maple syrup's in the air,
the shine of the street's reflected
in the backwash of the grill,
and some hulk of a guy in a hunter's vest
at the counter loudly reports
on last night's town meeting.
When he leaves the place gets quiet.

Outside again. No one's on the sidewalk.
Perhaps the cold keeps them in?
Or something else?
Then one old man comes from the north,
black overcoat, black stocking hat, tortoise shell cane
he taps on the walk like the Knock Code.
As he nears, he speaks, a low voice
as if you weren't entirely meant to hear.
And you don't, but you're certain
he has some message you must know.

Life's still here for sure—and history
even where the clock tower says *too late, too late*
and the abandoned paper mill stares at you
with its glassless eyes.
Where the ramshackle Victorian houses of the mill-rich

have become apartments, or rooming houses for the poor.
It's in the fossils found on the river bank,
and how you'll learn
that once, the Abenaki fished for salmon
in these ancient waters,
and how, beneath this street you're walking on,
hot springs bubble and steam,
how the whole town rests on them.

Watching the Night-Blooming Cereus Open

Seven white blossoms tightly folded
among the leaves on the viney stalks
that flow down five feet from the hanging planter.

Six old women in a semi-circle of chairs
chatting and watching on that one night
of the year the huge flowers would open.

Open so quickly we could almost see the unfurling.
Whatever fear we felt about aging,
we kept hidden from each other

as if in a pocket where long fingers
fold into a fist and then re-open.
Six old women chatting and watching.

When passion is long gone, still passion lingers.
How the buds opened, first to a pinwheel
then to the full white sheet of the flower.

How they performed for us
until cool midnight took its own gifts,
the flowers wilting, by morning the petals

all dropping to the plain wood floor.
Since that years-ago night, three of the women have died.
One is here, writing this. Does the cereus climb still

in that attic space? I want to think so.
In my own small rooms, I am remembering.
I keep the watchfire going.

THE GUEST

In the long July evenings,
the French woman
who came to stay every summer
for two weeks at my aunt's inn
would row my brother and me
out to the middle of the mile-wide lake
so that the three of us
would be surrounded by the wild
extravagance of reds that had transformed
both lake and sky into fire.
It was the summer after our mother died.
I remember the dipping sound of the oars
and the sweet music of our voices as she led us
in the songs she had taught us to love.
"Blue Moon." "Deep Purple."
We sang as she rowed, not ever wondering
where she came from or why she was alone,
happy that she was willing to row us
out into all that beauty.

AFTER "SNOW AT LOUVECIENNES,"
ALFRED SISLEY

A man trudges between eight-foot stone walls
    into the village of Louveciennes

along a path made of thick snow
                  and snow still falling

His long coat of black wool and his black hat
    and the black boots have walked him through
        many winters

The trees in the orchard
      just beyond the wall bend
          with the weight of snow

and the sky presses down its grays

He has been steeped in quiet for miles
    not even talking to himself
        His feet frozen to marble

snow stipples his cheeks
    But a friend has called him and wants him near

In the village beyond the screen of snow
    St. Martin's church hovers above the wall

From this cold path between
    what he's left behind and what will come

he hears the bells
        steeple bells
            ringing   ringing

BEGINNING OF WINTER—A SIJO SEQUENCE

Early December snow sifting down, as the light is leaving,
and I am watching the world darken from my window.
The one I am waiting for is not walking the white road to here.

＝

In late autumn I watched Monarch butterflies, migrating.
A thousand lights in the salt marsh fluttered over goldenrod.
A thousand waves of the sea broke beyond the scrub pines.

＝

Last night in the dream I was hungry, but there was no food.
I was thirsty and no one came near. Love was what I needed.
When I woke I returned to my desk and wrote down the dream.

＝

When the snow is falling like this, no birds sing in the ash trees
and nothing disturbs the ground, except the relentless snow.
I want only to stay inside where it is warm, on days like this.

＝

I've chopped onions, celery, carrots, and heated them in oil.
Three cans of tomatoes, one of chicken broth, I've dumped in the pan.
The soup will simmer an hour on the stove; it will taste good to me.

LETTER TO MY DOUBLE

Put away the golden mask. The closets are full now,
you will have to find another hiding place.
The wind will tell you where. Answers are all around you.
The gods are hidden in plain sight,
their bodies not concealed by the bushes.
Myths tell you everything you need to know
about the world—and nature says the rest.
What did Icarus think as he was falling into the sea?
That the sun was gold and splendid with fire,
that wax melts, that only birds were made for flying?
Except in dreams and planes, you are ground-born and tied.
Your feet connect with solid earth.
If you desired gold, you would be unhappy.
Your dreams tell you what you want:
a man's arms around your body, a safe place near water,
a bus that arrives on time to carry you home.

MESSAGE FOR THE DISHEARTENED

When you are expecting nothing
a letter arrives
and someone decides for you.
Your arms fall to your sides,
your hands open.

You dress for the weather
in your gold moccasins
and prepare for long journeys
to distant countries.

The foxes who come out of the forests
stall before you but do not startle.
They are so beautiful,
full of spice and sugar.

Vines grow wildly around you
tangling your thoughts.
There are so many countries
you've never traveled to.

You've been keeping
to your own rooms
like a blanket stored
inside a closet

or an Egyptian mummy
or a room full of model ships.
In case you miss me,
keep moving through time

and I will arrive finally
in a black coat and top hat,
leaving my cane in the closet,
to open your inner pages

saying, after all, life
is sweet and not as dangerous
as you might think—though the thief
runs off with the child before help comes.

AFTER THE MURDERS I DREAM
I AM WATCHING A RIDING LESSON

and the horses run away with the children
because a stranger, an aged man, suddenly shouts,
as he stands off by himself near the ring,
spooking the horses.
They jump the rails and gallop away
down the hilly street carrying the frightened
children, whose feet have lost the stirrups,
whose legs are flapping up and down
against the bodies of the horses.
The stranger has been told,
we (all of us watchers) have been told,
to be quiet, to be very still,
as the children practice their riding,
but the man is an angry man
or he is a crazy man, a devil,
or perhaps, I don't know, he is
in unimaginable pain.
He does not listen or else he does not hear
and so in the utter quiet of our watching
the children, one behind the other, trot around the field,
the man shouts out in rage
and we don't know how to stop the terror
as the horses rear and bolt under the wide-eyed children.

THE WOUNDED CLOWN, 1939

after the painting by Georges Rouault

Sad clown, his wife, their child.
They are, to each other, the world.
Behind them, night, hill, crescent moon, one tree.
The two lean close, hold hands,
beside the anxious child. The mood is blue.

And over the whole scene:
their bodies, the sky—a wash of blue
meant to give us the wounded world,
world at the edge of a war, captured
in downturned faces, the winter tree,

its unleaved limbs. The skeleton
of the three-branched tree
blacker than the grim night where no wind blows.
Sad clown, his wife, their child,
to each other they are the world.

Blue world, our world—these three, one dark hill, one bare tree.

AT CARMON'S FUNERAL HOME

In the half-light of two tall lamps, I lie bedded in satin,
as if on the stage of an amateur theatre.
My children weep (or don't) on folding chairs
while the few friends I have left
mill around whispering.
Near the double doors that lead back

into the world, someone laughs lightly.
Later, in the house I lived in, on the long table,
wine, tossed salads, cheeses, chicken casseroles.
Even now, I am puzzled by how,
in such solemn moments, survivors keep on
laughing, chatting, as if to say,

Whoa, death, we shall not succumb to you.
See how tomorrow calls to them
like the next page of a book
they can't stop reading. They turn away
and go and who am I to blame them.
I would rise and go with them if I could.

Plea to the Missing God

I am confined here living alone
indigent and like a snail.

They say you are loving. I salute you.
Here among the action of the wind

will your voice come to me?
Is it only echo, echo?

Will you say nothing
across the bones of what is hidden?

I am pregnant with words, please answer me.

I CAST A NET OVER SULLEN WATERS

1.

To make a song, my hands tug at the bounty
raising the four corners.

A storm blows over the lake from Thunder Mountain,
the boats speeding back to the pine-edged shore.

Rain on the roof of the boathouse
and at my aunt's inn, a fireplace filled with fire.

These were the happiest days of childhood:
perch the chef pan-fried for breakfast,

the ruined rec hall, its candlepin lane, beside the field
of Indian paint brush and white butterflies.

2.

About my infanthood, I have only
a few notes in a pale blue book

about nurses and formula, my mother's anemia,
how I took a first step in the '38 hurricane,

across the second floor apartment into a world
of my mother's applause and flood waters rising.

Beyond that innocence, in a far world, clouds
amassed in smoky rows

and dark birds scattered up
                              from the fields.

3.

So many languages, so many intricacies of each language,
and how are we to understand each other?

There is a door behind which no one goes. There is the last
underground river and a boat that carries the dead,

until even the sea wants to carry away its own name.

4.

The stars cast their insufficient light
into the universe.

Comes passion, and the brutality I try to keep out—
blood and torture, the madness we do to each other, the earth.

5.

The songs that continue to rise from our throats
begin again out of the fire,

out of the deaths and ghosts, out of the atrocities,
with acceptance, with denial or prayer—or with rage

so red-hot our hands shake from it, our throats dry out.
And still we begin again.

THE MESSAGE

The word came down from the mountain
into the valley, passing the tree line,

passing through the deciduous forest.
The stars that night were unforgiving

though they kept close to the valley.
Thin clouds partially obscured them, echoing

the message that carried with it the history
of your youth back from those days

you no longer remember.
Everything came clear at last

with the dawn sailing in
from offshore and landing on the lake

where shadows seemed to swim like otter-ghosts
through a country of darkness and light.

Then the shadows themselves disappeared,
skulking off toward the trees.

DREAMWORK

In my dream, I lay next to a man who was dying in a room
with many windows. I could feel the length of his body
against mine. I could feel the warmth of his breathing.

Our bodies seemed to flow one into the other
as if we were two small rivers that had merged
and widened out into one long shining.

Around us the poets were commenting
on each other's poems. I saw papers fluttering
as they passed them around. I could hear their voices

but not their words. Poems weren't important
to me anymore—only the man and his dying,
the stranger whom I loved because he was dying.

The poets went into the other room
for coffee and cakes, and I asked the man did he want
to be alone now, he told me no, stay here.

I shifted even closer to the life that was leaving.
When he seemed to be sleeping,
his breathing not regular anymore,

I rose and straightened the covers around him
and then I lay down on the bed again.
The man's body in its dying was a slim willow,

its leaves, gold and trailing.
He was supple and too young. He was quiet
for a long time, there was no struggle in him.

All day now, I keep trying to get back to the body
of the man in the dream, his quiet arms,
his side whose muscles relaxed against my side,

relaxed against my warmth.
I didn't know the man well enough to love him,
I don't know why I dreamed of him

but the bed in the dream enlarged to fill the whole room
and there was love there, not passion. What I imagine
a mystic feels when the God he believes in envelopes him.

All day, all day, images harden into ice.
It's winter. The rooftops are heavy with snow
and a sheet of wild yellow light.

GLOSA

*on lines from "In Memory of the Spanish Poet Federico
Garcia Lorca" by Thomas Merton*

Where the white bridge rears up its stamping arches
Proud as a colt across the clatter of the shallow river,
The sharp guitars
Have never forgotten your name.

I stood up to my knees in the April River
and the foam swirled like a lover around me
and didn't each species of bird and bush
blend into each other and didn't the sky come down
with its rose aurora as the clouds
descended in fragments and patches?
In the midst of all nature I stood there waiting
for you to come say your name in my ear.
I am the woman who sings and watches
where the white bridge rears up its stamping arches.

When I'd stood for hours saying prayers like wishes
when the gentle light had entered my body,
didn't you come on your ten-hands-high stallion
riding down the gorge from the farthest highlands?
I know that prayers have no real answers,
that the fabric of my faith's frayed but not riven.
Although you came to me, I couldn't understand you.
You brought no resolutions. Were you only a mirage?
Your mount, though, forged gamely into the silver
proud as a colt across the clatter of the shallow river.

As soon as you had come you galloped off in silence.
I was left on my own by the rapacious river
and how should I live then with no one to stay by me?
So I turned and left through the dark of the valley
and found a sad music in the fork of an ash tree,
a music made of wind and the tuning forks of stars.
I captured the notes and put them in my backpack,
carried the songs to play at the sad café, and there they spar
with a dancer on fire, and *the sharp guitars.*

Where the white bridge rears up its stamping arches,
once you came clattering on a pure black stallion.
You rode out of storm but you told me no answers;
you were dream and thunder, you never knew me.
When you rode away, I felt no transformation.
There was nothing and no one to blame.
Still there's something I reach for,
some lost part of my spirit I want to reclaim.
I've never forgotten your name.

When I Meet You

the forest will have broken open
its green gates to allow me in

and I'll walk through the undergrowth
as easily as if there had been a path there

though there is nothing but bramble,
briar, the scratching blackberry canes

how long, I wonder, have you been waiting

I will not know you are there but will walk quietly
expectantly in the direction of some secret voice

a voice I trust although I don't know
where it comes from or how it enters my hearing

when I meet you for the first time you will
step out in shielded light

surrounded by the cries of birds
and the harsh barks of foxes

what will be the sound of your voice I wonder
and how will I come to understand you

when I meet you
when I meet you for the first time

MAINTENANCE

Early morning's layer of snow, thin as wrapping tissue,
blue sky, scant white clouds,

                               one, ominous gray.
Eight birds, eight specks, fly over up high.
Wrought iron black fretwork of trees,
cold setting in with a glow like a ghost
silently on the ground,

                          the cars in the parking lot.
Frost scrim feathers the windows.
The maintenance man trudges by

                          with his pail and shovel.
The silent maintenance man.
Bringer of safety and solace, carrier of no news.
One pass at the walks is not enough.
He salts them again

                  then once for luck.
He doesn't see me watching him

                        from behind glass.
Cat curled in the wicker chair, layer of dust,
wax grapes and green wax pears in a clay bowl,
thick purple candle, metal table lamp with cutout heron,
bookcase stacked every-which-way with poetry,
seven paintings on the wall, gifts from artist friends.

Art and the ordinary.
What was given for pleasure and from which

                        pleasure is derived.
I give thanks.

                     ≈

In the snow of the new year,
the fur of the young century smooths down
releasing its electricity,

                    its sparks.

What will the year bring to the low table?
What plates of sorrow?
What platters (oh please yes!) of joy?
Is this a prayer or something like it I cast out?

               ≈

Once, in a dream I was painting the kitchen of an old house.
Just beyond it, in the high corner of the hall, a spider,
dressed in emerald and turquoise robes as if it were a god,

                            had spun its web.

It had a message that I couldn't hear
but its presence comforted me.

There are some dreams like that—
talismans, touchstones, gifts.

               ≈

Once I saw a fox caught in the lamplight
on the night lawn outside my apartment.
A fox! My totem. What message did he bring?
And once, I encountered a skunk waddling off

                    into the ornamentals,
leaving his footprints like letters across the snow.
And, of course, there are the birds
quieter now in the deep of winter.

              Or is it I who am quieter?

               ≈

Sunday now. Another day rising into dawn but so far
the sky is still dark as the inside of a coat sleeve.
No new snow, no new story.
The doctor said: *You should decide to participate in life.*
A friend said: *Your poems have become overwhelmed by mortality.*
I've been counting up my friends who've gone,
taking their energies and dreams. I've been told
some simply slid off at the very end,

       like ice on a hill, melting.

     ≈

Here the lamp lights the pad I write on.
Here three pens are scattered on the table.
Here is the dictionary where I retrieve words:
susurration, oneiric, phenomenology, chiaroscuro.
Here is my blood sugar testing kit,

       its strips and needles.
And here, the blue coffee mug Lucinda gave me
the year she died.

     ≈

Another day early, one window lit across the way.
As silent in here as the hush world of the near-deaf—

       such as I am.

Last night I gave a prayer up to the ether,
to the infinity, to the presence or absence,
to a cataclysm of creation and destruction

       beyond any I can imagine.
I asked for understanding, some hint of reason

       and continuance.

How lovely the overnight snow
                              illumined by the sidewalk lamp.
It turns to a blue radiance as the icy dawn light slips in
from the east, a chimeric light, a veil made of nothing.

SHADOW AT EVENING

After all day walking the Vermont craft fair in the sun
after the goat-milk soaps and rose-scented sachets
the bright pottery stalls and the wooden animals

while my shadow preceded me along the grassy aisles
and disappeared reappeared as I moved in and out
of the shadows of maples and gray ash trees

where the breathy music of the accordion player floated
where the field was vibrant with color and motion
stalls of candles relishes and pickles cotton candy in plastic sleeves

I drove home and my shadow rode beside me drove lazily
watching the Green Mountains pass outside the windows
home to my own small cache of solitude and grace

then my shadow disappeared into the brown carpet
disappeared into the bookshelves and the books
I never missed it but just continued on with my quiet life

but now through the east window evening approaches
but now night is knocking against the long shadows
of the street lamp as my shadow rises mysterious and compliant

and I beckon it to enter me until I am one with it at last
and I allow the day to close and dream to come
allow the dream to rise from nowhere and come to me

ACKNOWLEDGMENTS

Grateful acknowledgment is made to the editors and publishers of the following journals in which some of these poems first appeared.

Adana: "Father Poems: A Collage," "The Guest"
Alaska Quarterly: "Should the Fox Come Again to My Cabin in the Snow,"
    "The Precious Book"
Barrow Street: "After the murders I dream I am watching a riding lesson"
Cave Wall: "The Beginning of Winter: A Sijo Sequence"
Cerise Press: "The Letter," "The Wounded Clown, 1939"
Crab Creek Review: "After Snow at Louveciennes, Alfred Sisley," "Letter to
    My Double," "Sixty Years After My Mother's Death"
Green Mountains Review: "Depression"
Harvard Review: "Hunger"
Image: "Glosa," "When I Meet You for the First Time"
Naugatuck River Review: "Riding the Cog Railway up Mount Washington"
Nimrod International Journal: "Biography from Seventy-Four"
Poetry Daily: "Should the Fox Come Again to My Cabin in the Snow"
Poet Lore: "I cast a net over sullen waters," "when will the cows come
    home?," "Winter Grace," "At Allen Brothers Garden Center"
Poetry International: "Galway"
Tupelo Quarterly: "Winter," "Old Man Wearing Vegetation"
Valparaiso Poetry Review: "The Weight," "Dreamwork"

In addition, I would like to thank Sid Hall, Rodger Martin and Kirsty Walker of Hobblebush Books for accepting *Winter* and for the close attention they have made to every aspect of publishing it, and for their ongoing commitment to making beautiful books.

My thanks to Mary Oliver whose encouragement and whose own work continues to be an inspiration to me.

Thanks and gratitude also to Lana Hechtman Ayers, Susan Deborah King, Brenda Nicholson and Susan Roney-O'Brien, who read this manuscript in its many stages and made such insightful suggestions.

So many poets/friends have encouraged me, supported me and/or offered suggestions on the poems in *Winter.* Thank you to all of them. And especially to: Dorothy Anderson, Roderick Bates, Pam Bernard,

Polly Brody, Kathleen Fagley, Ann Fisher-Wirth, Ann Hostetler, Louisa Howerow, Ruth Karp, Meg Kearney, Jeffrey Levine (and the staff at Tupelo Press), Tim Mayo, Mary Jo Moore, Ardelle Osbourne, Alicia Ostriker, Gabriel Parker, Geri Radacsi, Pat Ryiz, Penelope Scambly Schott, Carole Stasioski, Shawn Supple, Jean Tandy, Jean Tupper, Roberta Visser, Herb Yood.

And lastly to my wonderful family whom I love very much and to Roger who was a loving presence in my life for over thirty years.

ABOUT THE AUTHOR

PATRICIA FARGNOLI is the author of six collections of poetry. Her last book, *Then, Something*, Tupelo Press, 2005 won the *ForeWord Magazine* Silver Poetry Book of the Year Award, co-won the New Hampshire Poetry Club's Sheila Mooton Prize and was an Honorable Mention for the Erik Hoffer Awards and a finalist for the New Hampshire Literary Awards. *Duties of the Spirit* won the 2005 NH Jane Kenyon Literary Award for an Outstanding Book of Poetry. Her first book, *Necessary Light* (Utah State University Press, 1999) was awarded the 1999 May Swenson Poetry Award judged by Mary Oliver. Her chapbook, *Small Songs of Pain* (Pecan Grove Press, 2003) is a collection of poems triggered by Chagall's illustrations of LaFontaine's fables. In addition she has published two other chapbooks. Patricia, who was the New Hampshire Poet Laureate from 2006 to 2009, is a retired clinical social worker, has been the recipient of a Macdowell Colony fellowship and has been a frequent resident at the Dorset Writer's Colony and Wellspring House. A past Associate Editor of *The Worcester Review*, she has been on the residence faculty of The Frost Place Poetry Festival, and has taught in the Lifelong Learning program of Keene State College and privately. She's been the recipient of an honorary BFA from The NH Institute of Art, has won the Robert Frost Foundation Poetry Award, been a semi-finalist for the Glasgow Book Award and three times a semi-finalist for the Discovery/The Nation award. A graduate of Trinity College, Hartford, CT, The Hartford College for Women, and the UCONN School of Social Work, Patricia has worked as a Research Analyst for the State Police, a YWCA program director with adolescents in trouble with the law, as an actuarial analyst and supervisor with Aetna Insurance Company, and most recently, for ten years prior to her retirement, as a psychotherapist in family service agencies. She has published well over 300 poems in anthologies and literary journals such as *Poetry, Ploughshares, North American Review, Mid-American Review, Harvard Review, Alaska Quarterly, Barrow Street, Images*, and *Rattle*. A member of the NH Writer's Project, The New England Poetry Club, and a Touring Artist for the NH Arts Council, she resides in Walpole, New Hampshire.

THE HOBBLEBUSH GRANITE STATE
POETRY SERIES

*HOBBLEBUSH BOOKS publishes several New Hampshire
poets each year, poets whose work has already received
recognition but deserves to be more widely known. The
editors are Sidney Hall Jr. and Rodger Martin.
For more information, visit the Hobblebush
website: www.hobblebush.com.*